CW00544768

Traverse Theatre Company
and Edinburgh International Festival
present

Meet Me at Dawn

by Zinnie Harris

First performed at the Traverse Theatre, Edinburgh,
on 6 August 2017

A Traverse Theatre Company Commission

The Company

Cast

HELEN
Sharon Duncan-Brewster
ROBYN
Neve McIntosh

Creative Team

Zinnie Harris	Writer
Orla O'Loughlin	Director
Fred Meller	Designer
Simon Wilkinson	Lighting Designer
Danny Krass	Composer & Sound Designer
Fiona Mackinnon	Assistant Director
White & Givan	Movement Advisers
Ros Steen	Voice Work

Production Team

Kevin McCallum	Production Manager
Renny Robertson	Chief Electrician
Claire Elliot	Deputy Electrician
Gary Staerck	Head of Stage
Tom Saunders	Lighting & Sound Technician
Gemma Turner	Company Stage Manager
Charlotte Unwin	Deputy Stage Manager
Shellie Barrowcliffe	Assistant Stage Manager
Sophie Ferguson	Costume Supervisor

Director's Note

from Orla O'Loughlin

'It is unthinkable to lose the one you love.'

Grief is like a tumble dryer. It turns our world upside down and inside out. The trauma sudden death creates has been likened to a grenade going off in the brain. It leaves our perception of who, what and where we are in bits.

The power of Zinnie Harris's writing lies in its clear-eyed confrontation with grief: an experience of shock, confusion and fear. But the joy of this play is that it manages yet to be an absolute celebration of our best selves. To experience deep loss is to have experienced deep attachment, and here we have love in all its giddy, intimate and sometimes maddening glory.

Meet Me at Dawn inhabits a thought experiment borne out of magical thinking: 'What if we had one more day?'

Above all *Meet Me at Dawn* is a love story, and the island, detached from the mainland forming a sort of liminal dreamscape, becomes the shimmering manifestation of Robyn's hopes and fears.

Although Robyn and Helen's grasp on what is real and what is not is slipping, what is never in doubt is their love for each other. And that is both the triumph and tragedy of this tidal wave of a play.

Orla O'Loughlin,
July 2017

Company Biographies

Sharon Duncan-Brewster (Helen)

Previous theatre credits include: *Swallow* (Traverse Theatre); *Nuclear War, Hope, Babies* (Royal Court Theatre); *A Streetcar Named Desire, So Special* (Royal Exchange Theatre); *The Iphigenia Quartet, Yerma* (Gate Theatre); *A Midsummer Night's Dream* (Liverpool Everyman); *The El Train* (Hoxton Hall); *The Swan, There is a War* (National Theatre); *Tiger Country, Keepers* (Hampstead Theatre); *Detaining Justice, Seize the Day, Category B, Let There Be Love, Fabulation, Playboy of the West Indies* (Tricycle Theatre); *The Horse Marines* (Theatre Royal Plymouth); *The Bacchae* (National Theatre of Scotland/Lincoln Center, New York); *Black Crows* (Clean Break/Arcola Theatre); *The Magic Carpet* (Lyric Hammersmith); *Blues For Mr Charlie* (Tricycle/New Wolsey); *Dirty Butterfly* (Soho Theatre); *Peepshow* (Frantic Assembly/Plymouth/Lyric Theatre); *Crave* (Paines Plough); *Yard Gal* (Clean Break/Royal Court/MCC Theater, New York); *The No Boys Cricket Club* (Stratford East Theatre Royal).

Television credits include: *Unforgotten, Cuffs, Cucumber, The Mimic, The Bible, Top Boy, Holby City, Casualty, Doctor Who, Eastenders, Doctors, Shoot the Messenger, Waking the Dead, Baby Father, Hope I Die Before I Get, Bad Girls, Body Story,* and *The Bill.*

Film credits include: *Rogue One: A Star Wars Story* (Lucasfilm/Walt Disney Pictures), *Three and Out* (Rovinge), *The Child* (Riders to the Sea Ltd) and *Blues for Nia* (BBC Film/Eclipse).

Zinnie Harris (Writer)

Zinnie Harris is a playwright, screenwriter and theatre director. Her plays include: the multi-award-winning *Further than the Furthest Thing* (National Theatre/Tron Theatre – winner of the 1999 Peggy Ramsay Award, 2001 John Whiting Award, Edinburgh Fringe First Award), *Oresteia: This Restless House* (Citizens Theatre/National Theatre of Scotland/Edinburgh International Festival 2017 – winner of Best New Play in Critics' Awards for Theatre in Scotland 2016), *How to Hold Your Breath* (Royal Court Theatre – joint winner of the Berwin Lee Award), *The Wheel* (National Theatre of Scotland – joint winner of the 2011 Amnesty International Freedom of Expression Award), *Nightingale* and *Chase* (Royal Court Theatre), *Midwinter* and *Solstice* (Royal Shakespeare Company), *Fall* (Traverse Theatre/Royal Shakespeare Company) and *By Many Wounds* (Hamstead Theatre).

Her stage adaptations include: Ibsen's *A Doll's House* for the Donmar Warehouse, and Strindberg's *Miss Julie* for the National Theatre of Scotland. Zinnie received an Arts Foundation Fellowship for playwriting, and was Writer in Residence at the Royal Shakespeare Company (2000 – 2001).

She has directed for the RSC, Traverse Theatre, Tron Theatre and Royal Lyceum Theatre, winning Best Director in 2017 Critics' Theatre Awards in Scotland for her production of Caryl Churchill's *A Number*. She has written for television including episodes for the BBC1 drama series *Spooks*, and two stand-alone television films for Channel 4. She is Professor of Playwriting and Screenwriting at St Andrews University, and an Associate Director at the Traverse Theatre.

Danny Krass (Composer & Sound Designer)

Current and upcoming credits include: *Who's Afraid of Virginia Woolf* (Rapture Theatre); *Without a Hitch* (Finland and touring).

Credits include: *International Waters* (Fire Exit); *Blackout* (Showroom/Tron Theatre); *Blackbird* (Citizens Theatre); *Who Cares* (Royal Court); *Milk, Swallow, The Devil Masters, Quiz Show, Spoiling* (Traverse Theatre); *Magic Sho, Josephine Bean, Huff* (Shona Reppe); *Kind of Silence, Smokies* (Solar Bear); *Pondlife, Martha, The Little Gentleman, The Voice Thief, White, Kes* (Catherine Wheels); *Up to Speed* (Imaginate); *My Friend Selma, Invisible Army* (Terra Incognita); *Robin Hood* (Visible Fictions); *My House, A Small Story* (Starcatchers); *Peter Pan* (Sherman Cymru); *Mikey and Addie, The Littlest Christmas Tree, Rudolf, Mr Snow, The Little Boy That Santa Claus Forgot* (Macrobert); *Skewered Snails, He-La* (Iron Oxide); *The Infamous Brothers Davenport* (Vox Motus/Royal Lyceum Theatre, Edinburgh); *One Thousand Paper Cranes* (Lu Kemp); *To Begin, The Tin Forest* (National Theatre of Scotland); *Sanitise* (Melanie Jordan).

Creator/director credits include: *Kind of Silence* (Solar Bear).

Fiona Mackinnon (Assistant Director)
Supported by the Federation of Scottish Theatre with funding from Creative Scotland.

Fiona Mackinnon studied directing at the Royal Conservatoire of Scotland.

Her directing credits include: *Flora's Fairy Challenge* (Beacon Arts); *Comedy of Errors, Mermaid* (Stanwix Theatre); *Summer Heart* (Tron Theatre); *I Can Get Along Without Shoes on my Feet* (The Arches); *Scape* (Chandler Theatre); *The City That Never Sleeps* (Fringe Theatre, Hong Kong); *Yellow Moon: The Ballad of Leila and Lee* (The Alma Tavern, Bristol and Edinburgh Festival Fringe).

She has also worked as Assistant Director on *Shall Roger Casement Hang?* (Tron Theatre); *Flora's Fairy Challenge* (Citizens Theatre); *Whatever Gets You Through the Night* (The Arches); *Tommy's Song, One Day in Spring* (Òran Mór); *King Lear, Kidnapped* (Royal Conservatoire of Scotland).

Fiona has also worked as a community director at the Bierkeller Theatre in Bristol, directing large-scale community projects, as well as running youth theatre workshops in Hong Kong, and working as a visiting practitioner at the University of Cumbria.

Fred Meller (Designer)

Notable theatre credits include: *A Number* (Royal Lyceum Theatre – nominated for Critics' Awards for Theatre in Scotland 2017); *Grain in the Blood, Milk, Swallow* (Traverse Theatre); *A Few Man Fridays* (Cardboard Citizens, The Riverside Studios); *Black Comedy* (The Watermill Theatre); *Woyzeck* (Cardboard

Citizens/Southwark Playhouse); *Alaska* (Royal Court); *Timon of Athens* (Royal Shakespeare Company/Cardboard Citizens/The Complete Works Festival); *The Fever* (Young Vic); *Pericles* (Royal Shakespeare Company/Cardboard Citizens); *The Whizz Kid, Caledonian Road* (Almeida Theatre); *The Visitation of Mr Collioni* (Platform Four Theatre Company/Salisbury Playhouse); *Life With An Idiot* (Gate Theatre/National Theatre Studio); *Variety* (Grid Iron/Edinburgh International Festival).

Fred is Course Leader for BA (Hons) in Performance: Design and Practice at Central Saint Martins, University of the Arts, London. She co-convened the Scenography Working Group at TaPRA (Theatre and Performance Research Association), and is a Senior Fellow of the Higher Education Academy and The Arts Foundation.

Fred trained at The Royal Welsh College and received an Arts Council Designers Bursary. She works on productions that are representative of the devised, collaborative and new writing agendas that are her concerns, and continues to work collaboratively for new writing and site-specific projects, alongside established texts in traditional theatres.

Fred has exhibited at The Prague Quadrennial in 1999 and 2003, winning the Golden Triga, and was selected to exhibit at The World Stage Design in Toronto 2005, and in the National Society of British Theatre Designers Exhibitions. Her work is also part of the V&A Museum permanent collection. Other awards include The Jerwood Design award and a Year of the Artist award.

Neve McIntosh (Robyn)

Theatre includes: *The Crucible* (Bristol Old Vic); *The Events* (Actors Touring Company); *Betrayal* (Citizens Theatre); *The Lady From The Sea* (Royal Exchange Theatre); *Proof, Run For Your Wife, When We Were Women* (Perth Theatre); *Three Women* (Edinburgh Fringe); *The Merchant of Venice* (Royal Lyceum Theatre, Edinburgh); *Great Expectations, Victoria* (RSC); *The Recruiting Officer* (Lichfield Theatre); *Don Juan* (Sheffield Crucible); *Outside On The Street* (Gate Theatre); *The Trick Is To Keep Breathing* (Tron Theatre); *The Barber of Seville* (The Arches).

Film includes: *Social Suicide, The Be All And End All* (Bruce Webb); *Salvage* (Lawrence Gough); *Spring 1941* (Uri Barbash); *One Last Chance* (Stuart Svaarsand); *Gypsy Woman* (Sheree Folkson); *The Trouble With Men and Women* (Tony Fisher); *Plunkett & Macleane* (Jake Scott); *The Leading Man* (John Duigan).

Television includes: *Shetland* (ITV); *Guerrilla* (Sky Atlantic); *The Replacement* (Left Bank Pictures); *Doctor Who, Death in Paradise, The Accused, Inspector Lynley Mysteries, The Hound Of The Baskervilles, Gormenghast* (BBC); *Critical* (Sky1); *Ripper Street* (Tiger Aspect); *Dracula* (Carnival Productions); *Case Histories* (Ruby Films); *Single Father* (Red Productions); *Inspector George Gently* (Company Television); *Psychos* (Kudos); *Sea Of Souls* (Carnival Television); *Low Winter Sun* (Tiger Aspect); *Ghost Squad* (Company Television); *Miss Marple* (LWT/ITV); *Bodies* (Hat Trick); *Trial & Retribution* (La Plante Productions); *Doc Martin* (Sky); *Lady Audley's Secret* (Warner Sisters); *Taggart* (STV).

Orla O'Loughlin (Director)

Orla is Artistic Director of the Traverse Theatre. Prior to taking up post at the Traverse, she was Artistic Director of Pentabus Theatre and International Associate at the Royal Court Theatre.

Directing work for the Traverse includes: *Girl in the Machine*, *Grain in the Blood*, *Tracks of the Winter Bear*, *Milk* (Tom Erhardt Award), Fringe First and Scottish Arts Club Theatre award-winning *Swallow*, Fringe First award-winning *Spoiling*, Fringe First, Herald Angel and CATS award-winning *Ciara*, *The Devil Masters*, *Clean*, *Fifty Plays for Edinburgh*, *The Arthur Conan Doyle Appreciation Society*, Herald Angel award-winning *Dream Plays* (*Scenes From A Play I'll Never Write*) and CATS nominated *A Respectable Widow Takes to Vulgarity* and *The Artist Man and the Mother Woman*.

Other directing work includes: *For Once* (Hampstead Theatre, National Tour); *Kebab* (Dublin International Festival/Royal Court Theatre); *How Much is your Iron?* (Young Vic); *The Hound of the Baskervilles* (West Yorkshire Playhouse/ National tour/West End); *Tales of the Country*, *Origins* (Pleasance/Theatre Severn); *Relatively Speaking*, *Blithe Spirit*, *Black Comedy* (Watermill Theatre); *Small Talk: Big Picture* (BBC World Service/ICA/Royal Court Theatre); *A Dulditch Angel* (National tour) and *The Fire Raisers*, *sob stories*, *Refrain* (BAC).

Orla is a former recipient of the James Menzies Kitchin Award and the Carlton Bursary at the Donmar Warehouse. She was listed in the Observer as one of the top 50 cultural leaders in the UK.

Her ongoing project *Locker Room Talk* by Gary McNair recently played at the Abbey Theatre, Dublin, Latitude Festival and will premiere as part of Traverse Festival 2017.

Ros Steen (Voice Work)

Ros has worked extensively in theatre, film and television. Work for the Traverse includes: *Grain in the Blood*, *Milk*, *Swallow*, *Ciara*, *The Artist Man and the Mother Woman*, *The Goat or Who is Sylvia?*, *The Last Witch*, *Damascus*, *Carthage Must Be Destroyed*, *Strangers Babies*, *Tilt*, *Shimmer*, *Dark Earth*, *Homers*, *Outlying Islands*, *Heritage*, *Knives in Hens*, *Passing Places* and *Solemn Mass for a Full Moon in Summer* (as co-director).

Other recent work includes: *306: Day*, *The James Plays* (tour), *Macbeth*, *Let the Right One In*, *Glasgow Girls*, *Black Watch* (National Theatre of Scotland); *Romeo and Juliet* (West Yorkshire Playhouse); *Cyrano de Bergerac* (Northern Stage/Royal & Derngate Theatre); *Travels with my Aunt*, *True West* (Citizens Theatre); *Hedda Gabler*, *Bondagers* (Royal Lyceum Theatre Edinburgh); *Death of a Salesman*, *Much Ado About Nothing*, *The Cheviot, the Stag and the Black Black Oil*, *Great Expectations*, *In My Father's Words* (Dundee Rep); *Blood Wedding* (Dundee Rep/Graeae/Derby Playhouse); *A Walk at the Edge of the World*, *Sex and God*, *Walden* (Magnetic North); *Expensive Shit* (Adura Onashile).

Television and film credits include: *God Help the Girl*, *I Love Luci*, *Hamish Macbeth*, *Monarch of the Glen* and *2,000 Acres of Sky*. Radio credits include: *East of Eden*, *Cloud Howe*, *The Other One* (BBC Radio 4). Ros is an Emeritus Professor of the Royal Conservatoire of Scotland.

White & Givan (Movement Advisers)

Previous choreography/movement work for the Traverse includes: *Girl in the Machine, Grain in the Blood, Milk, Tracks of the Winter Bear* and *Swallow*.

As performers and choreographers with over twenty-five years of experience, White & Givan Co-Artistic Directors Errol White and Davina Givan have a wealth of experience they have fed into the company since its inception in 2009 under its former name, Errol White Company. They have both performed internationally for many years, working alongside such distinguished directors and choreographers as Rui Horta, Darshan Singh Buller, Richard Alston, Wayne McGregor, Bob Cohan, and Janet Smith among many others.

In addition to their extensive performing and repertory work they are respected and valued education practitioners, having spent five years as Artistic and Creative Directors of National Youth Dance Wales, and have taught extensively across the UK. Since 2009 the company has received generous support from Creative Scotland, which has allowed Errol and Davina to share their artistic work and practitioner experience with the Scottish dance community. They've staged three successful and critically acclaimed Scottish tours of *Three Works*, *IAM* and most recently *Breathe*. They are currently engaged in a unique dance company in residence scheme with the University of Edinburgh.

Simon Wilkinson (Lighting Designer)

Previously for the Traverse, Simon designed the lighting for *Black Beauty, Grain in the Blood* and *Tracks of the Winter Bear*.

Other theatre designs include: *Dragon, The Infamous Brothers Davenport, The Not-So-Fatal Death of Grandpa Fredo, Bright Black* and *Slick* (Vox Motus); *The 306: Dawn, The Day I Swapped My Dad for Two Goldfish, Roman Bridge, Truant* and *A Sheep Called Skye* (National Theatre of Scotland); *Glory on Earth, The Iliad, The Weir, The Lion, The Witch and The Wardrobe, Hedda Gabler, The Caucasian Chalk Circle, The BFG, Bondagers, A Christmas Carol* and *Cinderella* (Royal Lyceum Theatre, Edinburgh); *God of Carnage* and *This Wide Night* (Tron Theatre); *Dr Stirlingshire's Discovery* and *Light Boxes* (Grid Iron); *Fisk, The Lost Things* and *Feral* (Tortoise in a Nutshell); *Mamababame* and *PUSH* (Curious Seed); *Pondlife* (Catherine Wheels); *Blow Off* (Julia Taudevin); *Dance of Death* (Candice Edmunds), *Grounded* (Firebrand); *Kora, Sex and God, Pass the Spoon, Wild Life* and *After Mary Rose* (Magnetic North); *After The End* and *Topdog/Underdog* (Citizens Theatre); *Chalk Farm* and *The Static* (ThickSkin).

Simon won, with Jamie Vartan, the 2015 CATS Award for Best Design for *Bondagers*. Over the years, his lighting has created a Guinness World Record, brought 30,000 people to a windswept Highland forest, and caused reports of an alien invasion.

Current projects: Vox Motus's *Flight* at the Edinbutrgh International Festival, and *Letters to Morrissey* at the Traverse Theatre.

About Traverse Theatre Company

The Traverse is Scotland's new writing theatre.

Formed in 1963 by a group of passionate theatre enthusiasts, the Traverse was founded to extend the spirit of the Edinburgh festivals throughout the year. Today, under Artistic Director Orla O'Loughlin, the Traverse nurtures emerging talent, produces award-winning new plays and offers a curated programme of the best work from the UK and beyond, spanning theatre, dance, performance, music and spoken word.

The Traverse has launched the careers of some of the UK's most celebrated writers – David Greig, David Harrower and Zinnie Harris – and continues to discover and support new voices – Stef Smith, Morna Pearson, Gary McNair and Rob Drummond.

With two custom-built and versatile theatre spaces, the Traverse's home in Edinburgh's city centre is a powerhouse of vibrant new work for, and of, our time. Every August, it holds an iconic status as the theatrical heart of the Edinburgh Festival Fringe.

Outside the theatre walls, it runs an extensive engagement programme, offering audiences of all ages and backgrounds the opportunity to explore, create and develop. Further afield, the Traverse frequently tours internationally and engages in exchanges and partnerships – most recently in Quebec, New Zealand and South Korea.

'The Traverse remains the best new writing theatre in Britain.'
(The Guardian)

For more information about the Traverse please visit

traverse.co.uk

With thanks

The Traverse Theatre extends grateful thanks to all those who generously support our work, including those who prefer their support to remain anonymous.

Traverse Theatre Supporters

Diamond – Alan & Penny Barr, Katie Bradford
Platinum – Angus McLeod, Iain Millar, Nicholas & Lesley Pryor, David Rodgers
Gold – Carola Bronte-Stewart, Helen Pitkethly
Silver – Judy & Steve, Bridget M Stevens, Allan Wilson
Bronze – Barbara Cartwright

Trusts and Foundations

The Andrew Lloyd Webber Foundation
The Backstage Trust
The Binks Trust
Bòrd na Gàidhlig
The Cross Trust
The Dr David Summers Charitable Trust
Edinburgh Airport Community Trust
The James Menzies-Kitchin Memorial Trust
The Linbury Trust
The Saltire Society Trust
Santander Foundation
The Souter Charitable Trust
The Unity Theatre Trust
The W. M. Mann Foundation

Corporate Supporter

Arthur McKay

Traverse Theatre Production Supporters

Cotterell & Co
Paterson SA Hairdressing
Allander Print
Narcissus Flowers

Special thanks go to

Edinburgh International Festival, Frances Thorburn, John Kielty, Blythe Duff, Brice Avery, Royal Lyceum Theatre Edinburgh, Alexandra Laurie, Katie Garner, Charlotte Moss, Craig Fleming, Catherine Wheels Theatre Company

Grant funders

ALBA | CHRUTHACHAIL

Traverse Theatre (Scotland) is a Limited Company (Registered Number SC 076037) and Scottish Charity (Registered Number SC 002368) with its Registered Office at 10 Cambridge Street, Edinburgh, Scotland, EH1 2ED

Traverse Theatre – the Company

EDINBURGH
INTERNATIONAL
FESTIVAL

The Edinburgh International Festival is an unparalleled celebration of the performing arts and an annual meeting point for peoples of all nations. Committed to virtuosity and originality, the International Festival presents some of the finest performers and ensembles from the worlds of dance, opera, music and theatre for three weeks in August.

Over the course of the year, the International Festival team travel the world in search of the most exciting and creative artists working today. Together, it brings unique collaborations, world premieres, new takes on classic works, critically acclaimed productions and more to captivate, thrill and entertain audiences from around the world. All in one place, right here in Scotland.

Find out more by visiting
eif.co.uk

Festival Staff

Fergus Linehan
Festival Director
and Chief Executive

Joanna Baker
Managing Director
and Company Secretary

Stephen Bremner
Technical Department
Administrator

Rob Conner
Finance Director

Carrie Cruikshank
Office Manager

Gillian Devlin
Ticketing Operations Manager

Elisa De Waal
Executive Assistant to the
Festival Director
(temporary contract)

Kirsty Dickson
Marketing Officer

Jane Dunbar
Head of Ticketing

Dean Dyer
IT Officer

Niki Furley
Head of Development

Roberto Garcia Pernas
Finance Manager
(temporary - job share)

Emma Hay
Creative Learning Officer

Miranda Heggie
Marketing Administrator

Sally Hobson
Head of Creative Learning

Jacqueline Howie
Finance Manager
(temporary - job share)

Louise Hutson
Individual Giving Manager

Jill Jones
Head of Artistic Management

Nicola Kenny
Digital Manager

Jennifer Kelley
Membership Officer

Rob Knight
IT & Database Manager

Adam Lavis
Senior Corporate Officer

Roy Luxford
Planning Director

Michael McGill
Senior Ticket Services Assistant

Andrew Moore
Head of Music

Fi Morley
General Manager, The Hub

Iwona Nabialek
Sponsorship
and Development Officer

Katie Paterson
External Affairs Coordinator

Marcin Potepski
Creative Artworker

Emma Rawson
Press Tickets Coordinator

John Robb
Head of Technical

Jonathan Rowbotham
Marketing Manager

Piotr Schmitke
Finance Officer

Jenny Searle
Chorus Manager

Brodie Sim
Creative Learning Project
Officer (temporary)

Kirsten Stewart
HR & Payroll Manager

Liz Wallace
Media Relations Manager

James Walsh
Ticketing Operations Manager

Jackie Westbrook
Marketing and
Communications Director

Jen White
Festival Programme Associate

Christopher Wynn
Development Director

Drew Young
Artists Co-ordinator

The Edinburgh International Festival would also like to thank the many temporary staff
who join the team as drivers, technical staff, box office, sponsorship staff and media team
for the Festival period each year.

Meet Me at Dawn

Zinnie Harris's plays include the multi-award-winning *Further than the Furthest Thing* (National Theatre/Tron Theatre; winner of the 1999 Peggy Ramsay Award, 2001 John Whiting Award, Edinburgh Fringe First Award), *How to Hold Your Breath* (Royal Court Theatre; joint winner of the Berwin Lee Award), *The Wheel* (National Theatre of Scotland; joint winner of the 2011 Amnesty International Freedom of Expression Award), *Nightingale and Chase* (Royal Court Theatre), *Midwinter*, *Solstice* (both RSC), *Fall* (Traverse Theatre/RSC), *By Many Wounds* (Hampstead Theatre) and *This Restless House* (National Theatre of Scotland/Citizens Theatre; Best New Play, Critics' Award for Theatre in Scotland, 2016). Her adaptations include Ibsen's *A Doll's House* for the Donmar Warehouse and Strindberg's *Miss Julie* for the National Theatre of Scotland. Zinnie received an Arts Foundation Fellowship for playwriting, and was Writer in Residence at the RSC, 2000–2001. She is Professor of Playwriting and Screenwriting at St Andrews University, and an Associate Director at the Traverse Theatre.

also by Zinnie Harris from Faber

ZINNIE HARRIS

Meet Me at Dawn

FABER & FABER

First published in 2017
by Faber and Faber Ltd
74–77 Great Russell Street
London WC1B 3DA

Typeset by Country Setting, Kingsdown, Kent CT14 8ES
Printed in England by CPI Group (UK) Ltd, Croydon CR0 4YY

A CIP record for this book
is available from the British Library

978-0-571-34124-5

2 4 6 8 10 9 7 5 3 1

Meet Me at Dawn was first performed at the Traverse Theatre, Edinburgh, on 6 August 2017. The cast was as follows:

Helen Sharon Duncan-Brewster
Robyn Neve McIntosh

Director Orla O'Loughlin
Designer Fred Meller
Lighting Designer Simon Wilkinson
Composer & Sound Designer Danny Krass
Assistant Director Fiona Mackinnon
Movement Advisers White & Givan
Voice Coach Ros Steen

Characters

Robyn

Helen

The play is set on a beach

MEET ME AT DAWN

Note on Punctuation

The spoken lines in this text start with a lower-case letter to stop each line reading like a statement; lines are often incomplete phrases, half-thoughts or utterances that pass from one to another, and are rarely whole sentences.

In general the spoken text is laid out according to each character's process of reasoning with each new line indicating a new thought.

A woman in her forties, Robyn, speaks to the audience.

Robyn   it seems to me, and I know nothing – I know
              less than nothing so anything I say you
              have to ignore really or pretty much
              pretty much anyway but it seems to me –
              in a time like this – in a place like this – that
              there is the first bit, that's to say the bit that
              comes now, the bit that comes before the
              rest but after the others, not the first bit then
              but the bit that is now
              and that bit is about asking a question
              and the questions is

              are you okay?

Helen   jesus

Robyn   are you okay?

Beat.

              Helen, Helen, are you okay?

Helen   yes I think

Robyn   bloody hell –

Helen   yes I think

Robyn   you're okay?

Helen   yes

Helen comes on to stage.

She is soaking wet.

Helen	yes fucking hell, yes I think
Robyn	I know
Helen	shit
Robyn	I know I know
Helen	I thought we were –
Robyn	we were
Helen	I mean I really thought –
Robyn	me too
Helen	fuck yes I'm alright are you?

The two women are both soaked through.

They look at themselves. There is a sort of giddy hysteria.

Robyn	yes I think
Helen	both fine?
Robyn	both fine
Helen	because I couldn't really –
Robyn	no, no –
Helen	I mean out there, in that place –
Robyn	I understand
Helen	every man for himself, or every woman – I was, there was a sort of cloud over my thinking and I couldn't, and I know I should have – I know I should have, you were there of course I knew you were struggling but –

Robyn   I was the same

They look at each other.

              I was the same, it's okay

Helen   I would have helped you if I could

Robyn   me too. I said it's okay

Helen   I would've swum back in for you
              I would've done anything for you
              it was just that –

Robyn   I get it

Beat.

              but look
              we're both okay
              does it matter? We're both okay

Helen looks at herself. Her arms and legs.

She laughs a bit.

Helen   yeah

She kind of whoops.

              yes yes

She whoops again.

              I'm kind of buzzing in fact, like my heart is
                going
              like it's going to come out of my ears or
                something
              do you think my heart might actually?

Robyn   I doubt it

Helen   like it's pumping louder or stronger or
              you could bottle this, you could actually sell this
              this this feeling
              like the strongest coffee or

Robyn   I'm not sure I like it

Helen   we could use it though? if we could keep this –
imagine if you could access this when you –
okay so you don't like it but imagine if you
could

Robyn   I thought we were properly

Helen   but imagine if you could train yourself, in
a meeting or
I can fucking rule the world
we could fucking rule the world
couldn't we?
if you could bring this up to order

Robyn   I thought we were –

Helen   hands feet
march or lift, lift a car or a house or
you know those stories, people lift houses
off children or
and now we know we are –
we can, this is in us too
all I am saying is
it's changed, we've changed, there's this
well it's amazing isn't it? We are going to
forget this
we shouldn't forget this
we should train this into our muscle memory

Robyn   I think I'm actually going to be sick

Helen   oh

Beat.

Robyn   sorry I know you are all – but
I feel dreadful

Beat.

Helen I'll find you something to vomit in

Robyn on the shore?

They look around.

Helen well what do you want?

Robyn I want to feel better
I want not to be wet
I want not to be shivering
I want that not to have happened
I want to be home
with you

Helen maybe you should take your clothes off
some of them
get your shoes off anyway
that jumper, it's holding the water
probably keeping you colder

Robyn aren't you cold?

Helen I'm like a furnace
yes alright cold a bit
but mainly – fucking hell

Robyn it will hit you in a minute
you're probably even colder than me but
  the shock

Helen I feel fine
I feel great
I feel – I am sorry that you don't feel all that
  good but

Robyn I feel like vomiting is that alright?
I mean I don't want to spoil what you have
  got with this great fucking feeling

Beat.

  sorry

15

Helen comes over.

Helen   no, I'm a moron

Robyn   I really think I'm going to vomit, I'm not
mucking about

Helen   I know

Robyn   don't rub my back

Helen   I wasn't going to

Beat.

it's the salt water isn't it?

Robyn   you're the scientist

Helen   salt water always makes you feel sick
if you swallowed some of that then –

Robyn retches.

She retches again.

Helen stands there looking spare.

Robyn   and don't watch me either
it's horrible to watch someone being sick

Helen   what am I supposed to do?

Robyn   find the way back to the car

Helen   can you walk?

Robyn   my feet aren't vomiting are they it's just my –
oh god

She retches again.

Helen looks around.

Helen   what do we do about the boat do you think?

Beat.

> sorry, concentrate on –
> you just

Helen looks over, out into the water.

> it's just we'll have to tell them won't we?

Robyn do we really have to talk about this now?

Helen no, sure
just we should tell them?
shouldn't we? get the money back,
damn thing wasn't seaworthy, might get
   a fat lot of compensation
the thing was too expensive anyway, I said
   that didn't I?

Robyn why did you say that word?

Helen what word?

Robyn compensation?

Helen they hired us a boat that sank, don't be stupid
we should at least get our money back
they probably saw anyway, they were probably
   laughing
two women like us, out in a boat?
I bet it looked hilarious

Robyn they won't have meant it

Helen of course they won't
but I bet it looked –
I bet it looked –
that is all I am saying, I bet it looked –
well we aren't made for –

Beat.

Silence for a second.

They look at each other.

Robyn you talk too much

Helen you love me

Robyn you drive me crazy

Helen crazy in a good way?

Robyn not always

Helen but sometimes?

Robyn sometimes, yes

Helen shrugs, playfully..

Helen there you go you see, sometimes,
sometimes sometimes, that is good enough
I drive you crazy, sometimes. What a fucking
   love poem
you ready to walk back to the car?

Robyn I suppose

Helen what's that?

Robyn where?

Helen you have something on you

Robyn oh

Helen there on your –
hang on

She sees something on Robyn's cardigan.

Helen nothing
just a –

Robyn well what?

Helen I don't know – a moth?

18

Robyn   let me see

Helen   it's like it's got tangled in your, wait a sec

She gets it off.

here

They look at it.

Robyn   poor fucker

Helen   pretty though

Robyn takes it.

Robyn   shouldn't even be here
should be inland
you don't get moths by the sea

Helen   I don't know

Robyn   you're the scientist

Helen   I study rocks, not living things

Robyn   it's a dead one

Helen   even still

Robyn holds it in her hand.

Robyn   what should I do with it?

Helen   put it down

Robyn   it's got beautiful red spots, one on each wing

Helen   what is wrong with you?
put it down yes

Robyn   maybe it flew on to me on the boat
maybe it was with me during all that
but then why isn't it wet?

She looks at it.

Helen	there is no meaning, there is no point trying to find meaning
	there is none. We had a horrible accident, a near miss. It's a dead moth
Robyn	how romantic you are
Helen	always
	my love poem back to you. It's a dead moth, pretty, yes, but a bit disgusting. Put it down

Robyn puts it down on the sand.

Robyn	something will eat it
Helen	yes
Robyn	red spots and all
	vomit it back up for its babies
Helen	almost certainly
	nature
Robyn	I guess
Helen	which way is the car?
Robyn	I thought you would know
Helen	not for certain

They both look around.

Robyn comes over.

Helen	not at all actually
Robyn	it was further back that boat place, it must be –
Helen	this isn't where we set off, is it?
	or is that . . .
Robyn	not exactly no but
	we're not even near

Helen looks around too.

Helen   we're further down the shore then
              must be, we must have –

Robyn   alright but which way from here?

Helen   there was a path
              there was a bridge
              a tree – you said if we went swimming later
                  we could hang our clothes on it

Robyn looks about.

Robyn   no trees here

Helen   well if we walk further around –

Robyn   no bridge

Helen stands up.

Helen   have you got your phone?

Robyn   of course not
              everything went down with the boat

They look around again.

Robyn   which is precisely because the second question,
                  after the first the first being after the
                  physical, is the physical okay? Then comes
                  where are we, the *where* being not just
                  geographically though that of course –
              the *where* being something has changed that
                  changed us
              are we as we were before and somewhere in
                  the dim recesses of something –
              somewhere in the dim is there a parallel us,
                  and where are they
              is there a parallel you?
              is there a parallel me? did something split there?

did we –?
she said muscle memory and the muscle
   memory, is the muscle memory of a place
   here or somewhere else or –
so the question is –

Helen   where the fuck actually are we?

They look at each other. They look around.

where the fuck actually are we?

They look again.

where the fuck?

Robyn   I heard you

Helen   you didn't answer

Robyn   take your fucking jumper off, you're getting
   hysterical

Helen   where the hell are we?

Robyn   I don't know
   what do you want, all the answers from me?
   I don't know okay. I don't know
   I'm as lost as you

They look again.

we went out in a boat
we got into trouble in the water
we're not good at boats

Helen   we were stupid to take it out

Robyn   we thought it would be nice
   romantic even

Helen   we sank

Robyn   we swam we –

Helen	this isn't where we left from
Robyn	okay so in our sort of muddle – while we were sinking we swam in an odd direction
Helen	maybe this is an island maybe we landed on an island
Robyn	what kind of island is there?
Helen	I don't know
Robyn	really?

Helen	it's just a suggestion, just an idea about
	    how come –
	you go up there, you can see the shoreline
	    snakes around
	does it snake around?
	this might even be a tiny island but

Robyn	we have no phone

Beat.

it doesn't really matter what size of island it is
we don't even know if it is an island –

Helen	of course not but –

Robyn	we have no phone, that's the point. We're on
	    a bit of land, we don't know where we are,
	    we are cold or likely to get cold and we have
	    no phone

Helen goes and looks at the bit of shoreline.

Helen	maybe we got carried down by the tide or something and this is just –
Robyn	what?

Helen	we walk in one direction as far as we can, see if it takes us back to here
Robyn	okay or
Helen	you have a better idea?
Robyn	we wait I suppose
Helen	we wait here?
Robyn	we find out what here is
Helen	you can see the shore, over there that must be the shore we came from, this is a kind of –
Robyn	you can hardly see it
Helen	you can see *something* is there you can see that something is there Robyn, fuck's sake look there is *something* there
Robyn	if you say so
Helen	maybe this is just a sandbank
Robyn	maybe it disappears at high tide you mean?
Helen	don't say that, no I didn't mean –
Robyn	we need to walk, we need to find out what it is
Helen	you can't fucking say there isn't anything there
Robyn	calm down
Helen	well look
Robyn	alright there is *something* there yes, there is where we came from but it doesn't do us any bloody good does it?

Helen	the sun is out
Robyn	and that means?
Helen	that means we aren't going to die of hypothermia
Robyn	while we are waiting to be drowned at high tide
Helen	we are going to warm up we might have to swim back, when we are ready
Robyn	I can't swim back, you can't swim back
Helen	we might have to do all kinds of things we didn't realise we would which is why it is lucky we have all this energy and power that we didn't think we could ever possess
Robyn	only I don't I feel sick
Helen	will you try Robyn please at least try

Beat.

Robyn	we could die of thirst
Helen	great trying
Robyn	well we could couldn't we? you can't drink the sea
Helen	we're only going to be here for a few hours
Robyn	you hope
Helen	someone – the people who own the boat the people who own the boat are going to say, shouldn't they be back in by now? they're going to look at their watches and go they should be back those women who took the boat out and who

we laughed at because we all knew they
didn't know what they were doing, you
know those women

Robyn   you said they were con men

Helen   they're going to want to know what happened
to their boat, aren't they? Con men or not
their boat is worth something, or they think it is
it went out with us on it
they're going to say what happened to those
women, at some stage
please try to be positive Robyn
the minute they've had that thought, we are
okay
they will phone someone, they will pick up
a phone
coastal rescue or something
someone will arrive in a speedboat with silver
blankets
they'll be thermoses and people and we'll
be okay

Robyn looks out to the shore.

Robyn   I can't really see it

Helen   why does that not surprise me?
bloody hell, it's there
there

Robyn peers.

you need your eyes tested

She peers again.

I've told you that before.

Robyn   there's a kind of smudge

Helen   that's where we came from, this, that is –

Robyn   it's a cloud

Helen   no it's a place it's a place where we have our
              car, and our home and our jobs and our
              bread that is mouldering in the bread bin
              and the bins that need emptying and a bed
              that needs clean sheets but is really fucking
              fantastic to sleep on
              and pillows and towels in the bathroom
              and the dog that belongs to our neighbour
              but is somehow ours
              and all the dirt on the kitchen floor and the
              crap we live with
              that's where it all happens

Robyn   maybe there is water here anyway –
              all this worry about being here

Helen   I'm not worried

Robyn   all this worry I have
              and there could be a stream just there

Helen   are you actually thirsty or are you –

Robyn   I am actually thirsty

Beat.

Helen   okay so I will find some water
              there really isn't much need for water since we
              will be here a really short time but
              you can survive days without water you realise
              that and I'm pretty sure you had water at
              breakfast, but
              yes if you need water
              maybe we should write 'help us' or something
              in the sand
              and then –

Beat.

They look at each other.

Then a pause.

Robyn   what are you doing?

Helen   what do you mean?

Robyn   you've stopped talking

Helen   I'm thinking

Robyn   you always talk

Beat.

Helen   I am thinking okay
is it not okay for me to think?

They both take a second to think.

        I'm thinking
        I'm still thinking

Pause.

It dawns on them that they are a bit fucked.

Robyn   there's actually a person

Helen   where?

Robyn   I think that is someone

Helen   can't see

Robyn   over there
look

Helen   it's a smudge

Robyn   a man I think or perhaps a woman

Helen   you said there was a smudge, that's a smudge
if ever I saw one

They both look.

	oh perhaps yes a woman
Robyn	thank you
Helen	and thank fuck
Robyn	why did you say that? we don't know what kind of woman it is it could be a weird woman, she could be –

Helen	does it matter if they are weird?
	a person will have a phone, man or woman
	   I don't care, another person
	it doesn't matter who it is, if there is a person
	   there is a phone
	isn't that right? Coastal rescue, they can ring
	   the coastal rescue
	in today's world, every person who isn't a baby
	   I suppose, I suppose not a baby but any
	   person has a phone –

Robyn	I don't have a phone
	she says
	the woman that we find
	
	and is it just me or is there something –?
	is there something about the way the skin fits
	   on her face or perhaps her eyebrows or –
	
	I don't have a phone she says again
	
	this is my precious Helen and this is a day and
	   somehow we are here and you, you have to
	   have a phone
	and I know I am muddled I know I am but –

Helen	what do you mean you don't have a phone?
Robyn	I don't have a phone, she says the same thing over and over
Helen	but that can't be –

Robyn	maybe she lives without a phone, people do Helen, people do live without a phone
Helen	out here? surrounded by sea
Robyn	all I'm saying –
Helen	okay okay, that's fine, no phone you don't have a phone how does one get off here? this place, how do you get off it?

Pause.

Robyn	she doesn't say anything – the woman
Helen	sorry, just do you know how to get back to the mainland? is there a causeway, does the tide go out?
Robyn	I don't have a phone she says
Helen	why does she keep saying that?
Robyn	I don't have a phone I don't have a phone
Helen	she's going on and on
Robyn	you're being rude
Helen	okay. Yes I see, we know you don't have a phone but do you know about the tide? I asked about the tide I didn't actually ask you about your phone
Robyn	you did ask that
Helen	before yes

now I am asking, how does one get off this
island?

Beat.

Robyn   she looks from me to Helen and back to me.

Helen   would you be able to help us?
we are trying to get off here?

Robyn   she says nothing

Helen   is it even an island, can you confirm this is
an island?
perhaps it isn't an island, perhaps you –

Beat.

how do you live here?

Robyn   she looks pretty cold and –

Helen   how can you live here?

Beat.

Robyn   maybe you're talking too fast, you're always
talking too fast

Helen   it's not too fast –

Robyn   I don't think she is following,

Helen   of course she is following, she understood
the first question
sorry but

Pause.

we have a dog, we are looking after it for our
neighbour, we have to get back for our dog.
even if not for ourselves, the dog is left
inside the house and we have to get off
this island

31

Robyn	maybe you are standing too close, there's something obviously a bit . . .
Helen	what?
Robyn	maybe you are crowding her
Helen	you try
Robyn	hi
	only we've been caught in a
Helen	only we've been caught in a
	she repeats you
Robyn	I can hear that she repeats me aha I see, yes but
Helen	aha I see, yes but
Robyn	okay
Helen	okay
Robyn	okay yes I get it you are copying
Helen	you are copying

Beat.

Robyn moves further away.

Robyn	she's crazy
Helen	I think we established that
Robyn	but she obviously isn't drowned, I mean the fact that she is here means on this whatever it is, that the tide clearly doesn't come in and sweep her away every night
Helen	well that's true
Robyn	something catches my eye

32

Helen	she's got your moth
Robyn	I can see that
Helen	she's picked it up
Robyn	it's not my moth, it doesn't matter if she has my moth does it
Helen	what happened to it?
Robyn	the woman says
Helen	what happened to it?
Robyn	it had nothing to do with us
I promise
is that the answer? Is that what she is looking for

and the parallel thing, the parallel thing and the moth –
there is something in muscle memory about the moth
the moth that should be wet but isn't
when she picks it up, I think I have seen this woman and this moth
I have seen the moth but not here
I have not been here before
but I have seen that moth
the women buries it slightly
then brushes her hands
she starts to walk away
now wait a minute
please don't just walk away, please as you are here and we are obviously in trouble –
tell us
how do you get off here? we really need some help
we seem to be trapped and as you are the only person |

              but she goes

Beat.

Helen   she knows every damn thing we are saying
              she knows every little thing
              she's doing this deliberately
              she's winding us up
              have you ever met a woman like that, prepared
                 to wind you up?

Robyn   she is unhinged in some way

Helen   of course she's unhinged
              but that doesn't excuse it

Robyn   there is a parallel day
              there is a parallel moth
              I am sure there is a parallel moth
              I have seen this moth before. This dry dead
                 moth
              it has two red spots. Helen is the person that
                 is more likely to know about what it is
                 for, but for some reason Helen isn't part
                 of this. This moment
              I don't know why Helen isn't but –
              I just look at the colour.
              there is a thing – what am I reaching for,
                 before the questions about who and where
                 was there
              a moment?
              a moth that was desiccated in the sun
              there was a moth one day – which day –
                 a moth that one day I found and
               someone said something
               someone said, yes
              someone said
               someone said
               no, someone said –

if I could just say what someone said, I realise
    I am . . .
someone said
if I could remember what someone said

Beat.

someone said
I had the moth in my hand, I was looking at
    the moth
just bear with me, someone said
someone said something
someone said something
they said something
something terrible
and I felt that sick
just like I felt now
someone said something terrible and I felt
    that sick

Helen   I'm not saying we shouldn't forget her I think
    we should stay as far away as possible but
if she knew she was winding us up
okay so we are on an island with a crazy
    woman but it doesn't matter because she
    doesn't look dangerous, though what would
    we know
she doesn't look like the sort to
I don't know what is the worst, she doesn't
    look like she is the sort to

Robyn   I feel really weird about this

Helen   what sort of weird?

Robyn   creeped out

Helen   don't be creeped out

Robyn   it's not just her though is it, it's being here

stuck –
I feel a sort of claustrophobic
like when you are locked in somewhere and
    can't get open the door

Helen   we won't be stuck for long

Robyn   we've no idea
we could be stuck for a week, the clouds are
    so low you can't even see where the shore is

Helen   I can

Robyn   it's a smudge

Helen   I don't know what you are talking about then,
    I don't know why you do this, yes it's not
    great, yes it's not even all that okay but what
    can we do, what is the point? you are almost
    dry now aren't you
we'll get back to the neighbour's dog
that is what you have to think, we will get
    back to her, that dog and our lives
this is shit and the day went tits up but

Robyn   there is a muscle thing
there is a muscle thing going on

Helen   please Robyn

Robyn   and you saw the moth first and

Helen   what are you talking about?

Robyn   I don't know Helen
I don't know but I am in my kitchen

Helen   our kitchen

Robyn   alright our kitchen only
fuck my head, my head is doing something
    weird

Helen   you are concussed maybe

Robyn   I am standing in our kitchen yes
              our kitchen or maybe my kitchen
              I am standing at the sink
              our sink fine, our sink, are you listening

Helen   yes I'm listening

Robyn   I am washing my hands because lately I have
              started to pick at the fingers the little bit
              between the nail and the finger, what is that
              part called, the bit by the nail anyway there
              is blood and the taps are running and all
              week I have been in and out and back and
              forward and in the car – our car – and even
              the people at reception know me and I have
              been there and the phone rings the phone
              rings Helen and my mother is in the room
              she has come to make sure I am okay, and
              she has persuaded me home, the only hour
              hardly I have been home since and I have
              just seen a dead moth on the windowsill
              and picked it up and the phone rings and
              the person says
              and the person says

Beat.

Helen   what? what did they say?

Robyn   you don't know?

Helen   you're starting to freak me out

Robyn   they said something about you

Helen   what about me?

Robyn   they said something about you, four little words
              they said

they said, this is my mother she has taken
   the call
and the water from the sink is running over,
   it's flowing over but no one is turning off
   the taps
I am not turning off the taps
you know how my mother hates to stand
   in our kitchen
the moth is in my hand
it's a particular moth and I remember thinking,
   while the water is running over, I must look
   it up I must find out what the moth is called
or Helen I should have asked Helen

Helen   what does she say?

Robyn   she says
she didn't make it
she says she didn't make it love.
she says –

Beat.

Helen   what the fuck are you on about?
are you trying to piss me off?
are you trying –

Robyn   no

Helen   you've gone as crazy as her, as that insane
   woman
I don't actually know what is going on here

Robyn   she says you didn't make it

Helen   so we are lost, we are in a bit of a pickle
   and you are saying all this nonsense you
   are saying

Robyn   I'm standing by the window in our kitchen,
   in front of the sink

Helen   stop it

Robyn   the water is overflowing

Helen   please just fucking stop it

Robyn   I see a dry moth on the windowsill, I pick it up

Helen   stop it

Robyn   I'm frightened

Helen   stop it

She thinks.

    okay
okay okay
you are frightened, we had a trauma
of course you are frightened, it was horrible
   I'm frightened
we nearly drowned but

Beat.

    so there is this thing –
first of all, and I am no doctor but
I think you've got concussion
I actually do, when I said it before it was
   just but –
I think you might have concussion Robyn
now that's serious and I'm not saying it
   isn't but –
first you were sick
we both saw you vomit
that's a sign of concussion isn't it?

Robyn   you didn't make it

Helen   will you stop saying that?

Robyn   that's what she said
         she took the call from the hospital, the senior

doctor
you aren't here –
we aren't here –
I am in my kitchen I think or
maybe I am in our bed which has become
    my bed

Helen   no

Robyn   everything that was ours has become mine

Helen   please stop saying this

Robyn   you aren't here

Helen   what the fuck do I do with that?
what the fuck am I supposed to do with that?
you've got concussion.

Beat.

listen
there are lots of things that happen when you
    bang your head
the boat rolled over
it was a stupid boat
I could see that you got hit as it turned,
    I could tell, I heard you cry out before –

Robyn   I was concussed
I was badly injured yes I think you are right
I think I was the worst off, I think there is
there is a second moment before the moth
I think there is a moment where we are got
    out of the water, the coastal rescue did
    come, everyone came and everyone was
    worried about me, I could tell they were
    worried about me and you were there

Helen   stop

Robyn   I got better
I was concussed and I got better
and you didn't
you had some sort of internal thing, bleeding
I rallied
you slipped

Beat.

Helen   what do you do when you are marooned on
    a tiny sand bank with your girlfriend and
    she starts to go crazy?
that is a question for you angels. Tell me what
    to do?
is there a handbook somewhere?
she is convinced we have been here before
    but she survived.
she survived, apparently I didn't
anyone any suggestion for that?

Robyn   I hope I'm going crazy

Helen   no doubt about it.
utterly bonkers

Beat.

             I'll get you some water
I am really not going to listen to much more
    of this. Jesus

Robyn   I feel really thirsty

Helen   there's something not right with you, okay.
    I'll get you help
I promise you I'll get you help
when the cloud clears, when I know how
    far we are from the shore
I have a toffee in my pocket. Bit soggy but
eat the toffee

	you need blood sugar, you've had a shock. Out there in the water was a body shock. I should have given you it ages ago.

Robyn   but I –

Helen   will you just eat the bloody sweet Robyn?
             just for once don't argue

Robyn   I don't like toffees

Helen   do what you are fucking told

Beat.

She hands Robyn the toffee.

Robyn eats it.

It's a bit soggy and tastes of the sea. Helen looks at Robyn to make sure she's eating it.

Beat.

Helen   my grandmother had this week where she
             utterly lost it
             maybe I never told you, I was a kid, eleven
             maybe
             did I tell you?

Robyn   not sure

Helen   she thought my grandfather was back, she
             was raving
             the staff in the home were devils
             it was frightening we were spirits or I don't
             know what we were, she screamed when
             she saw us
             honestly, she was hitting off the walls
             hallucinating and
             we thought that is it, she has gone, dementia
             or something

we'll never get her back, that's what we thought
my brother and I, she has gone
mum and dad in this hourly conference
turned out – few days later – it was a bladder
    infection
it was a bloody bladder infection
the infection in her blood
course of antibiotics, and she came back, later,
    utterly came back to herself
all I am saying is –

Robyn   she went that mad?

Helen   she went bonkers, then some medicine and
    right as rain

Robyn   is that true?

Helen   all I am saying

Robyn   can that happen?

Helen   all I am saying is something has happened
    with you
maybe you have an infection –

Robyn   I don't think –

Helen   maybe you hit your head
I think that's the most likely
maybe the water
do you have a headache?

Robyn   a bit

Helen   there we are then
concussion my bet, and whatever it is
we'll get it sorted

Robyn   it isn't a toffee it's a fruit pastel

Helen   even better

Robyn   it's a bit sweet

Helen   I wish I had another. I'd shove it down
                your throat

*Helen starts writing in the sand. She takes off her clothes
and lays them out.*

            rocks are easier than people, just in case you
                are wondering

Robyn   I wasn't

Helen   well they are

Robyn   what are you doing?

Helen   I am making an SOS sign that can be seen
                from the sky
            and don't shoot it down, don't tell me the
                million reasons why it won't work
            I need to do something

Beat.

Robyn   we could try that woman again

Helen   we could
            if we wanted
            we could try that woman again
            she is bonkers but go ahead

Robyn looks up.

Robyn   no one will see it

Helen   fuck's sake

Robyn   just saying, for them to see it they would have
                to be flying directly above

Helen   it is better to do something, isn't it? However
                futile. Another question for the angels,
                better to do something or not at all? Answer

that. To die trying, or to die from not trying?
Not that we are dying, it was a figure of
speech. How to use your energy. I think we
need to do something
someone will realise we are missing soon,
that's the thing, we have to remember the
people who own the boat, this is just in case

Robyn   I don't feel concussed

Helen   oh but I am dead?

Beat.

Robyn   maybe you aren't dead

Helen   you think?

Beat.

Robyn   I hope not

Helen   well that is something, thanks for that

Robyn gets up and puts her arms around her.

Robyn   of course I hope not

Helen   I get fed up with this

Robyn   with this what?

Helen   with this imagination
all this
this dark stuff
you, there is always something to worry about
something you are chewing at
nothing is ever just –

Robyn   that isn't true

Helen tries to push her off.

don't be so angry

Helen I'm not angry I'm just –
I'm really worried about you
I'm either worried or I'm really pissed off and I can't work out which one it is
get off me

Robyn please

Helen try not to be so crazy.
it was a horrible accident okay, but it didn't happen

She relents and hugs Robyn back.

Robyn kind of sobs.

it's okay
it's scary we have been through a trauma
it was horrible, when the boat went over it felt impossible to survive for a moment or two but –
and sure nothing like this ever happened to us before

Robyn it was just an accident. I know.

Helen exactly
and we did make it.

She goes back to her SOS sign.

when the cloud clears someone should be able to see this, I don't think they would have to be directly ahead
if they were in a plane over there or
maybe a birdwatcher with binoculars

Robyn maybe

Beat.

how much can you remember?

Helen of what?

Robyn	of the worst bit of the bit when –
Helen	not much
Robyn	slipping from the boat, fighting for breath
Helen	somehow getting to the shore feeling really buzzy then you vomiting
Robyn	under the water
Helen	nothing just as I say it felt hard to survive for a second then
Robyn	you do remember something –
Helen	no I don't I don't

She comes back over to Robyn and they kiss.

	I don't
Robyn	you must remember something, you said you were sorry you didn't help me
Helen	okay I remember that bit but

Beat.

Robyn	you promise you don't – because a second ago there
Helen	I promise I don't.

Beat.

Robyn	okay okay I imagined it the kitchen and the moth
Helen	you did imagine it

Robyn	the water pouring over the edge of the sink, the phone call –
Helen	of course
Robyn	maybe this is the real and the other is the unreal
	maybe as the boat went down and I could see you were in trouble and I couldn't help you, maybe it was then –
	maybe it was then I imagined standing in the kitchen and what it would be like if the worst happened and my mother would come round – of course she would and of course there would be trips back and forth to the hospital and of course they would know me in reception and maybe as I saw the moth, maybe it was at that point that it got lodged in my brain
	maybe the fucking utter terrible fear of what would happen as I saw you going underwater and knowing I couldn't help, maybe it was that fear that meant that I kind of fast-forwarded on that trajectory, that I went to the darkest place
Helen	you live your life in images I always said you should write or paint or something
Robyn	I'm an academic
Helen	you live in books, you deal in stories
Robyn	okay maybe I took that image, and when I saw the moth –
Helen	you live in the gothic novel that's why you are so miserable
Robyn	yes okay but can the brain do that?

Helen   yours can

Robyn   really? Project a horrible image, give you a
                  memory of something that never happened?

Helen   do you remember when we looked at that
                  house?
              the one by the river
              when you got your job

Robyn   vaguely

Helen   the one we put an offer in for, but didn't get

Robyn   it was a flat

Helen   it was on two floors

Robyn   it was tiny

Helen   we loved it, we would have loved it

Robyn   yes okay

Helen   remember the day, we went to the pub after,
                  we actually put the offer in from the pub
                  and we sat with a drink –
              we imagined every little detail of our lives
              we went over and over
              how we would climb the stairs at the end
                  of the day
              how we would kick off our shoes as we went
                  into the bedroom
              how we would watch the birds from the
                  kitchen window
              how we would make love in the living room
              how we would sit on the stairs with hot
                  chocolate and hot-water bottles listening to
                  the rain
              if we had a child
              remember we thought then we might have

a child –
we saw the child through the back
we could actually see –
I could imagine you working until late at
    night at the little table in the front room,
    I could image having to clear away our
    dinner things so you could work there
I could imagine what that place would be
    like so full to the brim with us

Robyn   yes

Helen   there are always parallel universes
every moment could split
I didn't die Robyn.
I got this surge of adrenalin
I was near to death but I got this incredible
    surge, this superhuman surge, and I swam
I swam

Robyn   what *is* that patch on your finger called?
I want to chew on it again but I try not to.
    I want to chew so much it is already
    bleeding
like I have taken it out on my finger
it's this patch beside the nail called and surely
    it's called something or maybe it doesn't
    need a name, maybe there is no reason for
    it to have a name except that when you have
    picked and picked and torn with your teeth
    for so many days when you go into the
    pharmacist and say I would like some cream
    you can say I would like some cream for this
    part, without having to show her the place
    where you have almost taken your own flesh
    off the bone
I am aware the woman is watching me

Helen is back on the shore, I have walked
    around I suppose. I suppose I must have
    walked around –
I don't remember walking around but Helen
    says I have concussion so everything is –
I look at the woman
she looks at me
I take a chair and sit down. There is a chair,
    I don't see why I shouldn't sit down
there isn't a name for the part of your finger
    beside your nail she says
there should be I say back and I am not
    surprised to hear her voice. Her voice is
    exactly as I thought
maybe she says, maybe there should be a name
    but there isn't
you aren't copying me now? I say
she looks at me she shrugs, she goes and gets
    a chair
she turns it the right way up
you bother me
you really bother me, I say to her
what do you want? she says
I want to know what you're doing here I say –
I want to know how you got here, and before
    you say I live here, or I belong here or any
    of that –
you don't
you don't belong here. I know where I saw
    you, I might have been temporarily, I might
    have for a second forgotten where I'd seen
    you and I might be pretending to Helen but –
it was the end of my garden
I saw you at the end of my garden
you turned up in a storm
don't look at me like that – she looks at me like

well she looks at me like she doesn't know
   what I'm saying, which is rot because of
   course she knows she knows every word
you came with a sleeping bag
you came with a bloody sleeping bag
you don't see as many women sleeping rough
   well you worry don't you so of course I said
   of course, there is a storm, please of course
   sleep in the garage, or where you want
I have never seen you before she says
what we never met?
is everyone crazy? Is everyone crazy around
   here? Is that the thing? I know I might have
   concussion but there are some things I
   know. I know I saw you
she shrugs
it's important to say this to her
you turned up at the end of my garden
our garden, only
the garden that became mine
you turned up in the middle of a bad storm
I saw you before. I said to Helen I said to
   Helen there is a person, a woman
I didn't say there is a woman I have seen before
I didn't say there is a woman who scares me
   a bit
no – bothers – me
there is a woman who came into my life after
   you went
there is a woman who said I could make a wish

She stops.

can you actually look at me when we are
   talking?
my whole life is falling apart
I don't know what I am doing here or where I

am supposed to be but
if I am supposed to be here
I don't want to go crazy
is this a kind of taunting, a kind of ridiculing
    me with is Helen alive or dead?
a kind of punishment for my grief?
I said I had seen you to the man I talk to
he isn't really a – well he is a kind of a
    counsellor
I'm not sleeping I see a counsellor
and this woman I told him, the first day I saw
    him
there was a storm and this woman with her
    sleeping bag
she came and slept in the garage
she scared me because she said she would
    give me a wish
and he said, the counsellor said, it sounds like
    someone from a book
the old woman with the sleeping bag
it sounds like a character, an archetype
and he knows I write about books so I said
    yes okay but this was real
and in the morning he said, when you went
    out to the garage, was she there?
and when I said no
he said it was a dream
you saw a woman that scared you, it was like
    a kind of shadow, your shadow, you saw
    what scared you in yourself
like if I fell through the gaps and didn't get
    over this
if I didn't get over this like everyone thinks
    I should or if I kind of fell to pieces and
    never found the way back then maybe
    I would be wandering with my sleeping bag

that is what he said
you're scared of being that women, that is all.
she's a gremlin, a scary figure, someone to
    not become
but I said, in the dream if it was a dream,
when the woman came with her sleeping bag
she said she would give me a wish
I wanted that wish I wanted that wish so badly
more symbols from a story he said
I wish I had never told him about the books
I would reorganise the universe and to hell
    with the consequences to have that wish,
    I said to him
I live here, she goes
on this island
but this place doesn't exist does it?
of course you live here
like you slept in my garden
three nights
second night I brought you some bread
so what I came to say, what I really came
    to say is
is this the wish? Because if this is the wish
    it's cruel, it's a joke it's horrible.
I don't want it. I don't want this wish.
take it back.

I want to go home Helen
I don't trust anything here.
if this is concussion, I don't like it.
I don't believe it, that is the main problem
I don't believe the ground is actually here
that the sun is shining.
you didn't make it
that is all I can think of
I know it's awful to say and believe me

it's been awful but –
I know you didn't make it because these
    months have been horrible and okay I hit my
    head and maybe you will say I am the totally
    fucking insane one but –
we went out on that boat, you didn't want
    to, it was my fault

Helen   shushh

Robyn   no
I couldn't remember it all at first, but little
    by little –
the condolence cards, the people smiling at me
    from across the street, the hideous memorial,
    the nights I couldn't sleep that I would have
    done anything

Helen   I've got help

Robyn   what?

Helen   there was a boat
just twenty minutes ago
I called you but
the clouds lifted just a bit and I could see
there was a boat out there
a little one, couple of people in it
I was like, here, we are marooned
they were so near I could shout
I was jumping up and down I was waving
    my arms

Robyn   you actually saw them?

Helen   they were so near

Robyn   there?

Helen   right there, you see. Someone is coming for us.
they will have seen that I was here and even

> if they couldn't get to me, they'll get help.

Robyn looks out to the water.

Robyn   are you sure?

Helen   yes

Robyn   what did they look like?

Helen   it looked like two women

Robyn   two women like us?

Helen   no just two women
I suppose a bit like us, but no
two women in a boat, they are going to help
    us, Robyn
will you please smile – ?
you said we had to find a way off here and
    I think I just did
I think we could be home by tomorrow

Robyn   tomorrow?

Helen   tonight, I mean tonight
we can get the dog and

Robyn   you said tomorrow –

Helen   well tonight or tomorrow

Robyn   are you okay?

Helen   I'm actually quite cold
I think the end of the adrenalin
I was jumping up and down, when I saw
    that boat
I think you were right, all that
I actually feel quite
we are looking after our neighbour's dog
    aren't we?

Robyn   come here
              yes we are looking after a dog

Helen   and the dog is called Rosie?

Robyn takes off her cardigan off and puts it around Helen.

Robyn   yes called Rosie
              you should have had the toffee

Helen   and it barks all night

Robyn   she barks all night

Helen   will you just believe me then please? For once.
              it doesn't always have to be you that knows
                  everything. I saw a boat and we are going
                  to get some help.

Beat.

Robyn   have you been sick?

Helen   no

Robyn   not at all?

Helen   not yet

Robyn   okay

Helen   my head is bleeding
              I didn't notice it before but –

Robyn   oh god

Helen   I think I, did I hit the boat?

Robyn   your hair got tangled in the motor
              christ Helen

Helen   my hair got tangled in the motor?

Robyn   that's what they said
              but it was the internal damage to your liver
                  that –

Beat.

Helen   I won't accept it

Robyn   neither you should

Helen   how can I accept it?

Robyn   of course you can't
how can you?
it's monstrous

Helen   impossible. Doesn't make sense

Robyn   that's what I said

Helen   it's utterly absurd, it's horrific it's, how could
it have happened?
we were out in a boat –
we were just larking around
it was an ordinary day

Robyn   don't accept it
I won't either

Helen   you can't have a day that starts as ordinarily
as ours

Robyn   I've got concussion, you've got concussion

Helen   it's not happening

Robyn   we won't accept it

Helen   and this, what is this?

Robyn   I don't know about this
I don't know about this

Beat.

Helen   would you put your arms around me?

Robyn puts her arms around Helen.

it can't be true anyway

Robyn	it isn't then
Helen	maybe we are both sick maybe we both got something in the water we have to remember my grandmother and her bladder infection
Robyn	absolutely.

Beat.

don't say anything else.

Helen	we always said we would be truthful
Robyn	okay
Helen	I do remember something from under the water or after

Beat.

I do have a sort of muscle memory
pain, my hair getting tugged

Robyn	my love

Beat.

Helen	can it really . . .?
Robyn	shush.

Beat.

Helen	it's so odd. I don't even feel like crying. I –

Beat.

I've got a question

Robyn	okay
Helen	I heard you talking to the woman crazy lady I heard you

Robyn   I don't know who she is

Helen   what was the wish?
if this is true then what was the wish?

Robyn   what?

Helen   you spoke to her about a wish, what was it?

Robyn   not important

Helen   tell me –

Robyn   stupid

Helen   we always said everything was honest between
us
what is the point if –

Robyn   I can't

Helen   why can't you?
we both know that we have concussion, at
least one of us has concussion, we can't trust
anything. What was the wish?

Robyn   a day

Beat.

Helen   a day?

Robyn   yes

Helen   you wished for a day?

Robyn   yes

Helen   a single day?

Robyn   don't get cross with me

Helen   you could have asked for a year, a bloody
lifetime, you asked for a day?

Robyn   I don't know why

Helen	we have a day?
Robyn	I didn't think it would actually happen, how could it happen
Helen	a fucking day
Robyn	don't get like that Helen it hasn't been easy
Helen	a teensy-weensy tiny day?
Robyn	I know it's
Helen	why not ask for a minute, a microsecond
Robyn	please stop
Helen	why not waste it totally, you get a wish and you throw it away?
Robyn	it wasn't a waste
Helen	wasn't it? christ alive a day! this is what this is. Our day?
Robyn	was there a boat?
Helen	don't change the subject
Robyn	I could still be concussed couldn't I?
Helen	you aren't concussed – I might be but you
Robyn	your grandmother then –
Helen	we both know what is going on here there's no avoiding it

Beat.

so what do we do, with this day?
this day you asked for
you asked for a day, and now you have it

Robyn	I don't want it
Helen	you don't want it?
Robyn	I didn't mean that I just meant –
Helen	is it a day in the middle of the accident, when it is over will we be back in the water?
Robyn	how should I know?
Helen	and then I get to die again?
Robyn	please stop.
Helen	my hair being ripped in the fucking motor, is that what happens?

Beat.

fucking hell
fucking fucking hell

Robyn	it's not enough, I know it's not enough
Helen	you're right, it's not enough
Robyn	it would never be enough even if I had asked for eighty years it wouldn't be enough
Helen	will I have to die again?
Robyn	don't ask me
Helen	I don't want to die again, if I already did it once
Robyn	I don't understand the rules
Helen	shit this is –

She starts to shake.

shit this is –

Robyn	please Helen

Helen	you shouldn't have done this
	other people get over grief, why do you
	have to be the one that can't stand it?

| Robyn | I wasn't saying I couldn't stand it |

Helen	everyone loses someone at some point
	don't they?
	this isn't a unique experience, everyone goes
	through the shit

| Robyn | I know – |

Helen	and I am not saying it wasn't bad but
	why do you have to be the one that finds
	it intolerable?
	why do you have to be the one that does
	all this?

| Robyn | I wasn't sleeping, I wasn't coping |

| Helen | for god's sake |

| Robyn | can't you find any sympathy? |

Helen	I am the one that is fucking *dead*. Sorry if
	my sympathy isn't completely focused
	around you.

Beat.

I'm just saying, it's quite extreme
it's quite an extreme thing to do
and I know it's been bad for you, but this, this
isn't exactly a picnic for me either
if I was – if I was what you said
then leave it
why not leave it?
why not fucking get over it?
why not leave me be?

| Robyn | I'm sorry |

Helen   jesus. You're sorry?

Beat.

She stands up.

you were always extreme
you say I talk too much but you –
any experience you had was always worse
you had a cold it was intolerable
you had a pain it was beyond coping
you had an exam it counted for twenty
    of mine –

Robyn   that isn't true

Helen   no wonder you couldn't do grief
no wonder!

Robyn   I fucking love you

Helen   I fucking love you too.
but this is, this –

Robyn   what?

Helen   this is fucked up

Robyn   yes this is fucked up
yes. Yes this is fucked up. Yes, do you think
    that you just dying wasn't fucked up?
do you think that you just walking out of
    here, ceasing to exist, do you think that
    wasn't utterly and totally against the laws
    of how things should have been? And do
    you think I haven't asked a few times why
    the fuck could you, how could you have
    done that?

Helen   I'm not saying

Robyn   no you listen to me –
do you think I haven't asked, raged, Helen

why the fuck couldn't you swim?
you don't go out in a boat if you can't swim,
    you don't fuck around over the side –
it wasn't an accident Helen you were mucking
    about

Helen we both were

Robyn I survived and you know what?
you left life in a total mess
there is no calm order that you left behind
    you totally utterly crapped on me
no will, no bank details, where the fuck
    have you left the key to your desk drawer
    you could start by telling me that –

Helen I can't remember

Robyn of course you can't you couldn't organise
        yourself when you were alive and yes maybe
        my experiences were extreme, maybe
        I worried about things a bit more but at
        least I got everything done
I have a will
I know my bank details. I have a file, if I had
        died, you would be able –
I didn't even have your mother's number, not
        that these things

Helen it's on the wall

Robyn in the hospital, do you think you should call
        her parents yes probably where the fuck
        is their number

Helen on the wall

Robyn it should have been on the wall, it wasn't
        on the wall
of course it should have been on the wall, that
        is where we keep all the numbers

it's not on the wall because it is to do with
  you, it is to do with *you* and therefore it isn't
  easy, it isn't possible for anyone else because
  all you ever thought about was yourself
  and hence you died
you died because you didn't fight hard enough
you didn't fight through it Helen and I will
  never forgive you –
you should have fucking fought, and swum
  and got your head out of that motor and
  told your liver not to pack in and bloody
  lived
you should have bloody lived.

Beat.

sorry but that is what I think

Pause.

Helen   fucking hell, so it's my fault?

Robyn   fuck it yes.

Beat.

Helen   I hate you sometimes

Robyn   I hate you too.
             the day you died, I was so angry.

Beat.

and don't think it's just me. We're all pissed
  off with you. Your mother
your brother is on antidepressants
your dad has hardly been out
but it's me, actually if you want to know
the one they are all worried about
I think I am fine but they think not
a woman comes to the garage at the bottom
  of the garden

66

our garden, the garden that has become mine,
    that has become only mine
our garden but it is mine now in a way I don't
    want
anyway a woman has come with her pathetic-
    looking sleeping bag and it is really fucking
    raining
and I know it is bad, and she is probably
    homeless, and I am worried about her,
    which I realise is a new thought, a thought
    that for once isn't about my fucking pain,
    yes Helen died but I can think about another
    person and I shouldn't do it but I say yes
    you could sleep in the garage, only the
    fucking garage of course I should have done
    it, yes you can sleep there –
and the next day I take her out bread and
    some tea and she says would you like a wish
and I fucking say yes Helen and okay I fuck it
    up because you know what I never thought
    it would happen
it can't happen
you can't get a day back
it's as impossible as you going in the first place
there is a strange place called grief and all the
    rules are changed.
so I made a wish
I fucking made a wish

Beat.

Helen   I don't like to hear of you not coping

Robyn   well get used to it

Helen   how bad is it?

Robyn   bad
lining up pills bad
not getting out of bed bad it's

Helen	still looking after the dog?
Robyn	not really
Helen	tell me you didn't have her put down –
Robyn	of course I didn't, I took her to a friend's
Helen	because she's not ours
Robyn	I know she's not ours she's with Toby
Helen	who's that?
Robyn	he lives further along the road, please don't forget everything
Helen	she'll come back fat
Robyn	she isn't coming back, she isn't our dog anyway the last thing I wanted was a dog to die on me, ours or not ours, and I forget all about her and to be honest I think she blames me she looks at me like, what the fuck is wrong with you?

Beat.

you don't know what it is –
extreme widowhood, you have no idea

Beat.

I didn't mean
I realise of course
but nothing ever happened to us as big as this

Helen	what now, if I tell you I am scared? Alright for you, you got your wish but –
Robyn	I don't know don't be, please don't be scared. I guess whatever it is, has already happened.

Beat.

Helen I won't be scared
but I am glad you at least realise that being
    scared is a possibility –
that being scared might in fact be normal,
    that it might not all be about you

Robyn I don't want you to be scared

Helen I don't want to be scared either, truth be told

Beat.

I'll try to remember where the key to my
    drawer is

Robyn thank you

Beat.

you know I didn't mean it

Beat.

Helen yes I know that.
but I didn't mean it either –
I certainly didn't mean it
it's fucking shit.

Robyn you could say that.

Beat.

Helen where do you think you are?

Robyn I don't know
in the house
I would say I am asleep but I don't sleep
I haven't been asleep even for a second I don't
    think for months –
I don't know where I am

I could be in the garden
I could be in the garage, she could have tied
   me up or I could be in bed
I suppose I am probably in the kitchen
maybe I am by the sink

Helen   where am I?

Robyn   I don't know that either

Helen   where am I Robyn?

Beat.

Robyn   you're in a grave
your mother wanted a grave
I said I thought you wouldn't mind, do
   you mind?

Helen   where is it?

Robyn   in her village
I don't go there much, I should go there more,
   to be honest I find your mother –
she asks what the hell we were doing out in
   a boat and I find I don't have an answer.
we were mucking about I suppose
we were treating life far too trivially and we
   got caught
we didn't realise that you shouldn't do anything
that you should stay inside that you should
   hang on to each other
that's what we should have done
stayed under our duvet not left our bedroom
never gone out –

Helen   my brother would never take antidepressants

Robyn   well he does now
he really does

Beat.

Helen	I'm not sure what I am supposed to do with all this –
	I don't actually know
	I don't actually, I mean what . . .?
Robyn	I don't know either
Helen	you don't get taught do you, you don't get prepared
	this isn't exactly
	I mean, one of those situations –

Beat.

	how much more of our day do you think we have got?
Robyn	a few hours?
Helen	fucking hell.

Robyn	and that's when you think about *when*
	and you realise how much worse it is to know that you are going to lose someone, that all those people that stay nights beside a bed or watch someone die from cancer, that their lot is worse because if it is unthinkable to lose the person you love, it is even worse to know that it is going to happen.
	and I know I don't get a second wish, of course you don't get a second wish. Who in the world of children's stories hundreds and hundreds of stories about wishes, whoever heard of someone who can get a second wish just because they didn't like how the first one turned out? But anyway I go and I find her and I ask –
	I find the woman, she is standing with her sleeping bag just like I first saw her in my garage

woman, I say, I don't care who you are or
    if you are a projection or my fear or a person
    in a story I haven't written yet but –
this is a nightmare, you brought me to a
    nightmare
this isn't a wish
if I am to be here and I am to be here with
    Helen then take away the muscle memory
please kind spirit or angel or please let me
    forget. Let me forget what is to come later.
let me be with Helen
let me be innocently with Helen on a beach.
take away everything I know if you need to,
    everything I ever learnt
because all I can smell is dying flowers, even
    when I move them all the whole world
    smells of dying flowers and this cardigan
    this widow's cardigan the only thing I can
    ever put on in the morning –
if this is to be with Helen then let it be a
    free day
free of all of that.
please whoever you are
if I have a wish, that is what I wish.

Nothing happens.

Robyn looks about.

    wish lady?

Helen has gone.

    Helen?
    Helen?

Robyn looks about her.

She looks panicked.

    no don't take her away –

I didn't mean
the counsellor said you were a figment of my,
   that I should argue with you, if he got that
   wrong or
okay I wasn't supposed to argue but I didn't
mean –
Helen?
Helen?
fucking hell Helen come back?

Helen?
I'll do anything, I'll tear up the universe,
   I'll start again
HELEN
I didn't mean it, I didn't mean to say I didn't
   want my wish, I just meant, to use the day
   you would have to not know, to be ignorant
   wouldn't you –?
I get it, you don't argue with wishes
I get it, you don't argue with the universe –
there is no argument
let me finish the day

She looks around.

Still nothing.

She looks around again.

More nothing.

please?
please –
so where am I, if she isn't here?
I'm in my bed –
I'm standing at my window –
I'm in the kitchen –
water is overflowing from the sink
why am I still here in this place?

alright I accept
is that what you want to hear?
I accept
she died
she died, she died hideously, and alone later
    in hospital
she died incrementally over days –
she got her hair caught in the motor and
    then mashed up her insides she
she fucking died, I wasn't there she fucking
    died
I accept
I accept
bring Helen back please
she fucking died
she is dead for ever and ever
I FUCKING ACCEPT
she is dead for ever and ever and ever and
    ever and ever
and I . . .

Helen comes back on. She is carrying some sticks.

Helen   the light is nearly fading, I thought we could
            make a fire.
            I found this old set, looks like it was a barbecue
                or something

Robyn   oh god

Helen   what?

Robyn   nothing
            I thought you'd gone that's all

Helen   I have.
            we know I have
            we might as well finish our sentences

Beat.

> but there are a few hours left

Robyn a few hours, is that all?

Helen a few hours is a few hours
it's a small thing but it is a thing
sit by the fire with me
if I can do this, you can

Robyn oh god

Helen shush. Nothing okay, we say nothing.

Robyn alright but
alright but

Helen alright.

Beat.

They say nothing.

Robyn how are you going to light it?

Helen what?

Robyn the fire. Two women lighting a fire
when have we ever been able to do something
    like that?

Helen ah ah, my discovery
we can't, we are rubbish at things like that
but we aren't *we* today.
I mean this isn't –
this is a place where the rules are fucked
a liminal place, a shimmer
I like toffees, you like fruit pastilles actually
    I would never have had a fruit pastille or
    a toffee in my pocket
when did I ever have a sweet in my pocket?
there wasn't an island here –

there wasn't an island there, if there was
   an island here we would've been okay
so I think we can probably light a fire
maybe with our fingertips or
look
matches
I have matches in my pocket of course I do
we could probably find a steak dinner if we
   looked hard enough in the sand
you want water –
there is water

Robyn   we couldn't do this before

Helen   we didn't realise where we were before
   we thought it was real

Robyn   and don't tell me there'll be a day when I will
   feel better and waking up and you not being
   there will even feel normal, and perhaps one
   day the sun will be out and I will hear birds
   again and fuck it I have read the books,
   I know that one day this –

Helen   shush

Robyn   is that why you are here? is that why this –
   to tell me that there are better things ahead,
   that I won't always feel like this and if so
   don't, don't say anything unless you have
   got a big mechanical arm that can reach up
   to the sun and roll it the other way around
   the world
   turn the clocks back

Helen   I've got nothing
   I've got nothing Robs
   I won't say any of that

Robyn   will it get better?

Helen   I don't know

Robyn   it's monstrous, every day
I have to crawl through the hours

Helen   it *is* monstrous
it shouldn't have happened

Robyn   it's a monstrous world, and it's not enough

Beat.

Helen   take the matches and light the fire
it's getting dark

Robyn   is that it?

Helen   yep
pretty much
the day will soon be over.